John Adams

Our Second President

Teri L. Tilwick

PEARSON

Boston, Massachusetts
Chandler, Arizona
Glenview, Illinois
Upper Saddle River, New Jersey

Illustrations
2 Joanne Friar.

Photographs
Every effort has been made to secure permission and provide appropriate credit for photographic material.
The publisher deeply regrets any omission and pledges to correct errors called to its attention in subsequent editions.

Unless otherwise acknowledged, all photographs are the property of Pearson Education, Inc.

Photo locators denoted as follows: Top (T), Center (C), Bottom (B), Left (L), Right (R), Background (Bkgd)

All Photos: Library of Congress.

ISBN-13: 978-0-328-67583-8
ISBN-10:   0-328-67583-0

11 12 13 V0SI 18 17 16 15

From Farm Boy to Lawyer

You may know that George Washington was our first president. But who was our second president? His name was John Adams. Like Washington, Adams was one of the **founders** of our country. The founders worked together to start the government of the United States.

John Adams was born in Braintree, Massachusetts, in 1735. Adams's father was a farmer, a shoemaker, and a leader of the community.

John Adams grew up on the farm, and loved to explore places. He liked to hike, skate, and swim. Adams wanted to be a farmer just like his father.

However, Adams's father told his son to stay in school and John Adams did. In fact, he went to Harvard College. After that, he taught in a one-room schoolhouse. Then he became a lawyer. He discovered that he liked speaking to groups of people.

Adams's first home

A Leader for American Freedom

In 1759, John Adams met Abigail Smith. Abigail was smart and cheerful. She also read a great deal and loved to write. John and Abigail married in 1764. When John Adams worked far from home, they wrote letters to each other.

Abigail Smith Adams

At this time, Great Britain ruled the thirteen **colonies**. Many people believed this was not fair. John Adams was one of them. He believed that people in the colonies should be able to rule themselves.

Adams wrote about freedom from Great Britain in a newspaper, the Boston Gazette. Then, John Adams met with other leaders in Philadelphia, Pennsylvania. The group was called the Continental **Congress**. The men decided to make a **declaration**. With the help of John Adams, Thomas Jefferson crafted it. The Declaration of **Independence** said that the colonies would no longer follow British laws. The declaration was approved on July 4, 1776.

Writing the Declaration of Independence

The War for Independence

The colonies had to fight Great Britain for freedom. They needed ships to fight the British at sea. Adams told Congress that America needed a navy. Congress listened.

In 1783, the war ended. The colonies had won their freedom. Soon after, General George Washington was **elected** the first president of the United States. John Adams was vice president.

In 1797, John Adams was elected the second president of the United States. Adams and his family were the first to live in the White House in Washington, D.C. John Adams said, "May none but honest and wise men ever rule under this roof."

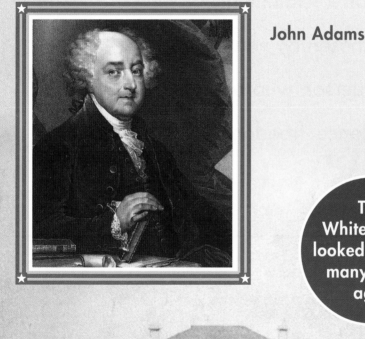

John Adams

The White House looked like this many years ago.

Glossary

colonies places ruled by another country

Congress group of leaders who gather to make laws

declaration a statement

elected chosen by voting

founder person who begins something

independence freedom